50 Best Idaho Cheese Recipes

By: Kelly Johnson

Table of Contents

- Idaho Potato and Cheddar Soup
- Baked Idaho Potato Skins with Cheese
- Idaho Potato Gratin with Gouda
- Cheddar-Stuffed Idaho Twice-Baked Potatoes
- Idaho Hash Brown Cheese Casserole
- Bacon and Cheese Idaho Potato Wedges
- Idaho Potato and Cheese Pierogies
- Cheddar Cheese Mashed Idaho Potatoes
- Cheese and Chive Idaho Potato Pancakes
- Idaho Loaded Baked Potato Casserole
- Idaho Potato Nachos with Melted Cheese
- Scalloped Idaho Potatoes with Gruyère
- Cheesy Idaho Breakfast Potato Hash
- Idaho Cheese and Corn Chowder
- Baked Mac and Cheese with Idaho Russets
- Cheddar and Broccoli Idaho Potato Bake
- Idaho Potato and Cheese Empanadas

- Cheese-Stuffed Idaho Potato Balls
- Idaho Red Potato and Feta Salad
- Idaho Cheddar and Ham Breakfast Bake
- Idaho Potato Cheese Fritters
- Creamy Idaho Potato and Cheese Soup
- Idaho Potato Gnocchi with Cheese Sauce
- Idaho Potato Tots with Queso Dip
- Cheddar and Bacon Idaho Potato Dip
- Idaho Potato and Cream Cheese Pierogi Casserole
- Parmesan-Crusted Idaho Potato Slices
- Idaho Potato and Cheese Quesadillas
- Idaho Blue Cheese Wedge Salad
- Cheddar and Onion Idaho Potato Bake
- Cheese-Stuffed Idaho Russet Bites
- Idaho Potato and Goat Cheese Tart
- Idaho Cheddar and Jalapeño Muffins
- Idaho Cheesy Potato Corn Cakes
- Gruyère Idaho Potato Galette
- Cream Cheese and Herb Idaho Potato Mash

- Idaho Potato and Cheese Breakfast Burritos
- Idaho Potato Cheese Chowder with Bacon
- Idaho Potato Pizza with Mozzarella
- Idaho Russet and Ricotta Fritters
- Idaho Potato and Asiago Gratin
- Cheddar-Stuffed Idaho Potato Loaf
- Idaho Cheesy Potato and Sausage Skillet
- Idaho Potato and Monterey Jack Tacos
- Cheese-Stuffed Idaho Potato Croquettes
- Idaho Red Potato and Cheddar Soup
- Idaho Baked Potato and Cheese Dip
- Idaho Potato and Blue Cheese Bake
- Idaho Cheese and Veggie Hash
- Idaho Cheddar and Garlic Potato Rolls

Idaho Potato and Cheddar Soup

Ingredients:

- 4 Idaho potatoes, peeled and diced
- 1 small onion, chopped
- 2 cloves garlic, minced
- 4 cups chicken or vegetable broth
- 1 cup heavy cream
- 1½ cups shredded sharp cheddar cheese
- Salt and pepper
- Chopped chives and bacon bits for garnish

Instructions:

1. In a pot, sauté onion and garlic until soft.
2. Add diced potatoes and broth; simmer until potatoes are tender.
3. Use an immersion blender to blend until smooth (or leave chunky).
4. Stir in cream and cheddar cheese until melted.
5. Season with salt and pepper. Garnish and serve.

Baked Idaho Potato Skins with Cheese

Ingredients:

- 4 large Idaho potatoes
- 1½ cups shredded cheddar cheese
- 4 strips bacon, cooked and crumbled
- 2 green onions, sliced
- Olive oil, salt, and pepper

Instructions:

1. Bake potatoes at 400°F (200°C) for 1 hour. Let cool, then halve and scoop out most of the flesh.
2. Brush skins with oil, season, and bake for 10 minutes.
3. Fill with cheese and bacon. Bake 5–7 minutes more until cheese melts.
4. Top with green onions.

Idaho Potato Gratin with Gouda

Ingredients:

- 4 Idaho potatoes, thinly sliced
- 1½ cups shredded Gouda
- 1 cup heavy cream
- 2 garlic cloves, minced
- Salt, pepper, and nutmeg

Instructions:

1. Preheat oven to 375°F (190°C).
2. Grease a baking dish. Layer potatoes, seasoning each layer with salt, pepper, nutmeg, garlic, and cheese.
3. Pour cream over top. Cover and bake for 45 minutes. Uncover and bake 15 minutes more until golden.

Cheddar-Stuffed Idaho Twice-Baked Potatoes

Ingredients:

- 4 large Idaho potatoes
- 1 cup shredded cheddar cheese
- ¼ cup sour cream
- 2 tbsp butter
- Salt and pepper
- Chives for garnish

Instructions:

1. Bake potatoes at 400°F (200°C) for 1 hour. Cool slightly, then cut in half and scoop into a bowl.
2. Mix potato flesh with cheese, sour cream, butter, salt, and pepper.
3. Refill skins and bake at 375°F (190°C) for 15–20 minutes. Garnish with chives.

Idaho Hash Brown Cheese Casserole

Ingredients:

- 1 bag frozen hash browns (thawed)
- 1½ cups shredded cheddar cheese
- 1 can cream of chicken soup
- 1 cup sour cream
- ½ cup melted butter
- Salt, pepper, and paprika

Instructions:

1. Preheat oven to 350°F (175°C).
2. Combine all ingredients in a large bowl and mix well.
3. Spread in a greased casserole dish.
4. Bake for 40–45 minutes until bubbly and golden.

Bacon and Cheese Idaho Potato Wedges

Ingredients:

- 4 Idaho potatoes, cut into wedges
- 1 cup shredded cheddar cheese
- ½ cup cooked bacon bits
- Olive oil, salt, pepper, garlic powder

Instructions:

1. Toss wedges in oil and seasonings.
2. Bake at 425°F (220°C) for 25–30 minutes, flipping halfway.
3. Top with cheese and bacon, bake 5 minutes more until melted.

Idaho Potato and Cheese Pierogies

Ingredients (Dough):

- 2 cups flour
- 1 egg
- ½ cup sour cream
- Pinch of salt

Filling:

- 2 cups mashed Idaho potatoes
- 1 cup shredded cheddar cheese
- Salt and pepper

Instructions:

1. Mix dough ingredients, knead until smooth, chill 30 min.
2. Roll out dough, cut circles.
3. Mix filling, place spoonful in each circle, fold and seal.
4. Boil pierogies for 3–4 minutes. Optionally, pan-fry in butter after boiling.

Cheddar Cheese Mashed Idaho Potatoes

Ingredients:

- 4 Idaho potatoes, peeled and cubed
- ½ cup milk
- ¼ cup butter
- 1 cup shredded cheddar cheese
- Salt and pepper

Instructions:

1. Boil potatoes until tender, then drain.
2. Mash with milk, butter, salt, and pepper.
3. Stir in cheddar cheese until melted and smooth.

Cheese and Chive Idaho Potato Pancakes

Ingredients:

- 3 Idaho potatoes, peeled and grated
- 1 egg
- ¼ cup flour
- 1 cup shredded cheddar cheese
- 2 tbsp chopped fresh chives
- Salt and pepper
- Oil for frying

Instructions:

1. Squeeze excess moisture from grated potatoes.
2. Mix with egg, flour, cheese, chives, salt, and pepper.
3. Heat oil in skillet, form mixture into small patties.
4. Fry until golden on both sides. Serve hot.

Idaho Loaded Baked Potato Casserole

Ingredients:

- 4 large Idaho potatoes, baked and cubed
- 1½ cups shredded cheddar cheese
- ½ cup sour cream
- 4 strips bacon, crumbled
- 2 green onions, sliced
- Salt and pepper

Instructions:

1. Preheat oven to 375°F (190°C).
2. In a bowl, mix potatoes, sour cream, cheese, bacon, and green onions.
3. Pour into a greased casserole dish.
4. Top with extra cheese and bake for 20 minutes.

Idaho Potato Nachos with Melted Cheese

Ingredients:

- 4 Idaho potatoes, sliced thin
- Olive oil, salt, pepper
- 1½ cups shredded cheese (cheddar, Monterey Jack)
- Optional toppings: sour cream, green onions, jalapeños, bacon bits

Instructions:

1. Toss potato slices with oil, salt, and pepper.
2. Bake at 425°F (220°C) for 25–30 minutes until crisp.
3. Arrange on platter, sprinkle cheese and toppings.
4. Bake until cheese melts. Serve hot.

Scalloped Idaho Potatoes with Gruyère

Ingredients:

- 4 Idaho potatoes, thinly sliced
- 2 cups heavy cream
- 2 cloves garlic, minced
- 1½ cups shredded Gruyère cheese
- Salt, pepper, and nutmeg

Instructions:

1. Preheat oven to 375°F (190°C).
2. Layer potatoes in a greased dish with garlic, cheese, and seasonings.
3. Pour cream over top.
4. Cover and bake for 45 minutes, then uncover and bake 15 minutes more until golden.

Cheesy Idaho Breakfast Potato Hash

Ingredients:

- 3 Idaho potatoes, diced
- ½ onion, chopped
- 1 bell pepper, chopped
- 1 cup shredded cheese
- 2 tbsp butter or oil
- Salt, pepper, paprika

Instructions:

1. Sauté potatoes in butter until golden.
2. Add onion and bell pepper, cook until soft.
3. Season and stir in cheese until melted.

Idaho Cheese and Corn Chowder

Ingredients:

- 3 Idaho potatoes, peeled and diced
- 1 cup corn (fresh or frozen)
- 1 small onion, chopped
- 2 cups milk
- 1 cup shredded cheddar cheese
- Salt, pepper, butter

Instructions:

1. Sauté onion in butter. Add potatoes, corn, and milk.
2. Simmer until potatoes are tender.
3. Stir in cheese and season. Blend partially if desired.

Baked Mac and Cheese with Idaho Russets

Ingredients:

- 2 cups cooked elbow macaroni
- 2 medium Idaho potatoes, cooked and mashed
- 2 cups shredded cheddar cheese
- 1 cup milk
- 2 tbsp butter
- Salt and pepper

Instructions:

1. Preheat oven to 375°F (190°C).
2. Mix macaroni with mashed potatoes, cheese, milk, butter, salt, and pepper.
3. Spread in baking dish and bake 20–25 minutes.

Cheddar and Broccoli Idaho Potato Bake

Ingredients:

- 3 Idaho potatoes, diced
- 1½ cups broccoli florets
- 1 cup shredded cheddar cheese
- ½ cup milk
- 2 tbsp butter
- Salt, pepper

Instructions:

1. Boil potatoes and broccoli until just tender.
2. Mix with cheese, milk, butter, salt, and pepper.
3. Bake at 375°F (190°C) for 20–25 minutes until bubbly.

Idaho Potato and Cheese Empanadas

Ingredients:

- 2 cups mashed Idaho potatoes
- 1 cup shredded cheddar
- 1 tsp garlic powder
- 1 package empanada dough (or pie crust rounds)
- 1 egg (for egg wash)

Instructions:

1. Preheat oven to 375°F (190°C).
2. Mix mashed potatoes, cheese, and garlic powder.
3. Spoon filling onto dough rounds, fold and seal edges.
4. Brush with egg wash and bake 20–25 minutes until golden.

Cheese-Stuffed Idaho Potato Balls

Ingredients:

- 2 cups mashed Idaho potatoes
- 1 cup shredded cheese (cheddar or mozzarella)
- 1 egg
- 1 cup breadcrumbs
- Salt and pepper
- Oil for frying

Instructions:

1. Form mashed potatoes around small cubes of cheese into balls.
2. Roll in egg, then breadcrumbs.
3. Fry until golden and crisp. Serve warm.

Idaho Red Potato and Feta Salad

Ingredients:

- 2 lbs Idaho red potatoes, cubed
- ½ cup crumbled feta
- ¼ cup olive oil
- 2 tbsp lemon juice
- 2 tbsp chopped parsley
- Salt and pepper

Instructions:

1. Boil potatoes until tender, drain and cool.
2. Toss with feta, olive oil, lemon juice, parsley, salt, and pepper.

Idaho Cheddar and Ham Breakfast Bake

Ingredients:

- 4 cups diced Idaho potatoes
- 1 cup cooked ham, cubed
- 1½ cups shredded cheddar
- 6 eggs
- ½ cup milk
- Salt and pepper

Instructions:

1. Preheat oven to 375°F (190°C).
2. In a greased dish, layer potatoes, ham, and cheese.
3. Beat eggs with milk, salt, and pepper. Pour over.
4. Bake for 30–35 minutes until set.

Idaho Potato Cheese Fritters

Ingredients:

- 2 cups grated Idaho potatoes
- 1 cup shredded cheese
- 1 egg
- ¼ cup flour
- Salt, pepper
- Oil for frying

Instructions:

1. Mix potatoes, cheese, egg, flour, and seasonings.
2. Heat oil and drop spoonfuls of mixture into skillet.
3. Fry until golden on both sides. Drain and serve.

Creamy Idaho Potato and Cheese Soup

Ingredients:

- 4 Idaho potatoes, diced
- 1 small onion, chopped
- 2 cups chicken or vegetable broth
- 1 cup milk or cream
- 1½ cups shredded cheddar
- Salt, pepper, butter

Instructions:

1. Sauté onion in butter, add potatoes and broth.
2. Simmer until potatoes are soft.
3. Stir in milk and cheese, blend slightly if desired.

Idaho Potato Gnocchi with Cheese Sauce

Ingredients:

- 2 cups mashed Idaho potatoes
- 1 cup flour
- 1 egg
- 1½ cups cheese sauce (cheddar or Gruyère based)

Instructions:

1. Mix potatoes, flour, and egg into dough.
2. Roll into ropes, cut into gnocchi pieces.
3. Boil until they float. Drain, toss with cheese sauce.

Idaho Potato Tots with Queso Dip

Ingredients:

- 2 cups grated Idaho potatoes
- ½ cup shredded cheese
- ¼ cup flour
- Salt, pepper
- Queso dip (store-bought or homemade)

Instructions:

1. Mix potatoes, cheese, flour, salt, and pepper.
2. Form into small tots. Bake or fry until golden.
3. Serve with warm queso dip.

Cheddar and Bacon Idaho Potato Dip

Ingredients:

- 2 cups mashed Idaho potatoes
- 1 cup shredded cheddar
- 4 strips bacon, crumbled
- ½ cup sour cream
- 2 green onions, sliced

Instructions:

1. Mix mashed potatoes, cheese, sour cream, bacon, and green onions.
2. Warm in oven or microwave.
3. Serve with chips, crackers, or veggie sticks.

Idaho Potato and Cream Cheese Pierogi Casserole

Ingredients:

- 12 lasagna noodles (or cooked pierogi dough)
- 3 cups mashed Idaho potatoes
- 1 cup cream cheese
- 1 cup shredded cheddar
- 1 sautéed onion
- ½ cup sour cream
- Butter for topping

Instructions:

1. Preheat oven to 375°F (190°C).
2. Mix mashed potatoes with cream cheese and onion.
3. Layer noodles, potato mixture, and cheddar in a casserole dish.
4. Top with sour cream and butter.
5. Bake 25–30 minutes until golden.

Parmesan-Crusted Idaho Potato Slices

Ingredients:

- 4 Idaho potatoes, sliced thin
- ½ cup grated Parmesan
- 2 tbsp olive oil
- Salt, pepper, garlic powder

Instructions:

1. Preheat oven to 400°F (200°C).
2. Toss potato slices with oil and seasoning.
3. Press one side into Parmesan.
4. Bake Parmesan-side up on a lined sheet for 25–30 minutes.

Idaho Potato and Cheese Quesadillas

Ingredients:

- 2 cups mashed Idaho potatoes
- 1½ cups shredded cheese (cheddar or Monterey Jack)
- 1 tsp cumin
- Tortillas
- Butter for grilling

Instructions:

1. Mix potatoes, cheese, and cumin.
2. Spread on half a tortilla, fold, and grill with butter.
3. Cook until golden and cheese is melted.

Idaho Blue Cheese Wedge Salad

Ingredients:

- 1 head iceberg lettuce, quartered
- ½ cup Idaho potato croutons (small roasted cubes)
- ½ cup blue cheese crumbles
- ¼ cup bacon bits
- Blue cheese dressing

Instructions:

1. Plate lettuce wedges.
2. Top with potato croutons, blue cheese, bacon, and dressing.

Cheddar and Onion Idaho Potato Bake

Ingredients:

- 3–4 Idaho potatoes, sliced
- 1 onion, thinly sliced
- 1½ cups shredded cheddar
- ¾ cup cream
- Salt, pepper

Instructions:

1. Preheat oven to 375°F (190°C).
2. Layer potatoes, onions, and cheddar in a baking dish.
3. Pour cream over the top.
4. Bake covered for 30 minutes, then uncovered for 20 more.

Cheese-Stuffed Idaho Russet Bites

Ingredients:

- 3 large Idaho russet potatoes, baked and cooled
- Cubed cheese (cheddar, mozzarella)
- 1 egg
- 1 cup breadcrumbs
- Oil for frying

Instructions:

1. Scoop out potato flesh, form around cheese cubes into balls.
2. Dip in egg, roll in breadcrumbs.
3. Fry until golden and melty inside.

Idaho Potato and Goat Cheese Tart

Ingredients:

- 1 pie crust
- 3 Idaho potatoes, thinly sliced
- 4 oz goat cheese
- 2 tbsp cream
- Fresh thyme, salt, pepper

Instructions:

1. Preheat oven to 375°F (190°C).
2. Spread goat cheese mixed with cream on crust.
3. Layer with potato slices, thyme, salt, and pepper.
4. Bake 30–35 minutes until golden.

Idaho Cheddar and Jalapeño Muffins

Ingredients:

- 1 cup grated Idaho potato
- 1½ cups flour
- 1 cup shredded cheddar
- 2 eggs
- ½ cup milk
- 1 diced jalapeño
- 1 tbsp baking powder
- Salt

Instructions:

1. Preheat oven to 375°F (190°C).
2. Mix all ingredients into a thick batter.
3. Divide into greased muffin tin.
4. Bake 20–25 minutes until golden and puffed.

Idaho Cheesy Potato Corn Cakes

Ingredients:

- 2 cups grated Idaho potatoes
- 1 cup corn kernels (fresh or frozen)
- 1 cup shredded cheddar
- 2 eggs
- ¼ cup flour
- Salt, pepper, and chives

Instructions:

1. Mix all ingredients into a thick batter.
2. Heat oil in a skillet. Drop spoonfuls and flatten.
3. Cook 3–4 minutes per side until crispy and golden.

Gruyère Idaho Potato Galette

Ingredients:

- 3 Idaho potatoes, thinly sliced
- 1½ cups shredded Gruyère
- 2 tbsp melted butter
- Salt, pepper, and fresh thyme

Instructions:

1. Preheat oven to 400°F (200°C).
2. In a cast-iron pan, layer potatoes, seasoning, and cheese.
3. Press down, brush with butter.
4. Bake for 40–45 minutes until crisp and golden.

Cream Cheese and Herb Idaho Potato Mash

Ingredients:

- 4 Idaho potatoes, peeled and cubed
- ½ cup cream cheese
- ¼ cup butter
- ¼ cup milk
- Chopped chives and parsley
- Salt and pepper

Instructions:

1. Boil potatoes until tender. Drain.
2. Mash with cream cheese, butter, and milk.
3. Stir in herbs, season to taste.

Idaho Potato and Cheese Breakfast Burritos

Ingredients:

- 2 cups diced and roasted Idaho potatoes
- 4 scrambled eggs
- 1 cup shredded cheese (cheddar or Monterey Jack)
- Tortillas
- Salsa or hot sauce (optional)

Instructions:

1. Warm tortillas.
2. Fill with potatoes, eggs, and cheese.
3. Roll and toast in a skillet until golden.

Idaho Potato Cheese Chowder with Bacon

Ingredients:

- 4 Idaho potatoes, diced
- 4 strips bacon, chopped
- 1 small onion, diced
- 2 cups broth
- 1 cup milk or cream
- 1½ cups shredded cheese (cheddar)
- Salt and pepper

Instructions:

1. Cook bacon, remove and set aside.
2. Sauté onion in bacon fat. Add potatoes and broth.
3. Simmer until tender. Add milk and cheese.
4. Blend partially for a creamy texture. Top with bacon.

Idaho Potato Pizza with Mozzarella

Ingredients:

- Pizza dough
- 2 Idaho potatoes, thinly sliced
- 1½ cups shredded mozzarella
- Olive oil, rosemary, salt

Instructions:

1. Preheat oven to 450°F (230°C).
2. Roll dough, brush with oil.
3. Top with potato slices and mozzarella.
4. Sprinkle rosemary and salt. Bake 12–15 minutes.

Idaho Russet and Ricotta Fritters

Ingredients:

- 2 cups grated Idaho russets
- ¾ cup ricotta cheese
- 1 egg
- ¼ cup flour
- Salt, pepper, and garlic powder

Instructions:

1. Combine ingredients into batter.
2. Drop spoonfuls into hot oil and fry until golden.
3. Drain on paper towels and serve warm.

Idaho Potato and Asiago Gratin

Ingredients:

- 3–4 Idaho potatoes, thinly sliced
- 1 cup shredded Asiago cheese
- 1 cup heavy cream
- 1 garlic clove, minced
- Salt, pepper

Instructions:

1. Preheat oven to 375°F (190°C).
2. Layer potatoes, cheese, and cream in a greased dish.
3. Bake for 40–45 minutes until bubbly and browned on top.

Cheddar-Stuffed Idaho Potato Loaf

Ingredients:

- 2 cups mashed Idaho potatoes
- 1½ cups shredded cheddar
- 1 egg
- ½ cup breadcrumbs
- 1 tsp garlic powder
- Salt and pepper

Instructions:

1. Mix mashed potatoes, egg, breadcrumbs, garlic, salt, and pepper.
2. Flatten mixture, add cheddar to center, then shape into a loaf.
3. Bake at 375°F (190°C) for 30–35 minutes until golden and firm.

Idaho Cheesy Potato and Sausage Skillet

Ingredients:

- 3 cups diced Idaho potatoes
- 1 lb sausage (crumbled)
- 1 cup shredded cheese (cheddar or blend)
- 1 diced onion
- Salt, pepper, and paprika

Instructions:

1. Cook sausage in a skillet, remove and set aside.
2. Sauté potatoes and onion until golden.
3. Return sausage, sprinkle cheese, cover, and melt.

Idaho Potato and Monterey Jack Tacos

Ingredients:

- 2 cups cooked diced Idaho potatoes
- 1 cup shredded Monterey Jack
- Small flour tortillas
- Sour cream, salsa, cilantro (optional)

Instructions:

1. Warm potatoes in a skillet.
2. Fill tortillas with potatoes and cheese.
3. Heat in a pan until tortillas crisp and cheese melts.

Cheese-Stuffed Idaho Potato Croquettes

Ingredients:

- 2 cups mashed Idaho potatoes
- ½ cup shredded cheese
- 1 egg
- ½ cup breadcrumbs
- Oil for frying

Instructions:

1. Form mashed potatoes around a small cube of cheese.
2. Roll in egg, then breadcrumbs.
3. Fry until golden and serve hot.

Idaho Red Potato and Cheddar Soup

Ingredients:

- 4 Idaho red potatoes, diced
- 1 onion, chopped
- 3 cups broth
- 1 cup milk or cream
- 1½ cups shredded cheddar
- Salt and pepper

Instructions:

1. Sauté onion, add potatoes and broth. Simmer until soft.
2. Blend slightly for texture, stir in milk and cheese.
3. Heat through and serve warm.

Idaho Baked Potato and Cheese Dip

Ingredients:

- 2 large Idaho baked potatoes, mashed
- 1 cup sour cream
- 1 cup shredded cheddar
- ½ cup bacon bits
- 2 green onions, chopped

Instructions:

1. Mix all ingredients.
2. Bake at 375°F (190°C) for 20 minutes until bubbly.
3. Serve with chips or bread.

Idaho Potato and Blue Cheese Bake

Ingredients:

- 3 Idaho potatoes, thinly sliced
- ½ cup crumbled blue cheese
- ¾ cup cream
- Salt, pepper, and nutmeg

Instructions:

1. Layer potatoes in a greased baking dish.
2. Pour cream over, top with blue cheese.
3. Bake at 375°F (190°C) for 35–40 minutes until golden.

Idaho Cheese and Veggie Hash

Ingredients:

- 2 cups diced Idaho potatoes
- 1 zucchini, diced
- 1 bell pepper, diced
- 1 cup shredded cheddar
- 1 tbsp oil

Instructions:

1. Sauté potatoes in oil until almost tender.
2. Add veggies, cook until soft.
3. Stir in cheese until melted and serve.

Idaho Cheddar and Garlic Potato Rolls

Ingredients:

- 2 cups mashed Idaho potatoes
- 2 cups flour
- 1 tsp baking powder
- 1 cup shredded cheddar
- 1 tsp garlic powder
- Salt

Instructions:

1. Mix all ingredients into a soft dough.
2. Shape into rolls, place on a baking sheet.
3. Bake at 375°F (190°C) for 15–18 minutes until golden.